Richard M. Nixon

Jimmy Carter

Ronald Reagan

E D M U N D   L I N D O P

TWENTY-FIRST CENTURY BOOKS
A Division of Henry Holt and Company
New York

Twenty-First Century Books
A Division of Henry Holt and Company, Inc.
115 West 18th Street
New York, NY 10011

Henry Holt® and colophon are trademarks of
Henry Holt and Company, Inc.
Publishers since 1866

Library of Congress Cataloging-in-Publication Data
Lindop, Edmund.
Richard M. Nixon, Jimmy Carter, Ronald Reagan / Edmund Lindop. — 1st ed.
p. cm. — (Presidents who dared)
Includes bibliographical references and index.
Summary: Chronicles the lives of presidents Nixon, Carter, and Reagan and points
out daring measures each took while in office.
1. Presidents—United States—Biography—Juvenile literature. 2. Nixon, Richard
M. (Richard Milhous), 1913–1994—Juvenile literature. 3. Carter, Jimmy, 1924–
—Juvenile literature. 4. Reagan, Ronald, 1911–   —Juvenile literature. 5. United
States—Politics and government—1945–1989—Juvenile literature. [1. Nixon,
Richard M. (Richard Milhous), 1913–1994. 2. Carter, Jimmy, 1924–   .
3. Reagan, Ronald, 1911–   . 4. Presidents. 5. United States—Politics
and government—1945–1989.] I. Title. II. Series.
E176.1.L5267 1996
973.92'092'2—dc20   95–33192
[B]   CIP
                                                             AC

ISBN 0–8050–3405–6
First Edition 1996

Printed in the United States of America
All first editions are printed on acid-free paper ∞.
10 9 8 7 6 5 4 3 2 1

Cover design by Robin Hoffman
Interior design by Kelly Soong

Photo credits
Copyright by White House Historical Association,
photographs by National Geographic Society:
Cover (left) and p. 8: *Richard M. Nixon* by J. Anthony Wills
Cover (center) and p. 24: *Jimmy Carter* by Herbert E. Abrams
Cover (right) and p. 40: *Ronald Reagan* by Everett Raymond Kinstler

For Gwen, Courtney, and Meredith Seamon

CONTENTS

This book discusses Richard M. Nixon, the thirty-seventh president; Jimmy Carter, the thirty-ninth president; and Ronald Reagan, the fortieth president.

President Nixon dared to visit Communist China and pave the way to restoring normal relations, which had been cut off for over twenty years. He also promoted an easing of tensions with the Soviet Union. However, Nixon became the only president to resign from office, which occurred because of his role in the sordid Watergate affair.

President Carter backed a treaty that gave Panama the right to assume full control of the Panama Canal in 1999. Carter also dared to bring together the heads of the governments of Israel and Egypt. Their discussions led to an end to the lengthy state of war between these two countries.

President Reagan dared to sign a treaty with Soviet leader Mikhail Gorbachev in 1987 that provided for the mutual destruction of some types of nuclear missiles, thereby lowering the world's arsenal of nuclear weapons for the first time. Reagan also brought sweeping changes to the American economy, although his program resulted in a huge increase of the national debt.

RICHARD M. NIXON

Richard Milhous Nixon won more votes for president than any other in U.S. history (113 million votes in three elections). He was the only man ever to be elected twice as vice president and twice as president. Yet this remarkably successful politician also was the only president to resign from office in disgrace.

Nixon's first memory was of falling—and then pulling himself up and running. He was three years old, and his mother had taken him riding in a horse-drawn buggy. Suddenly the horse turned a corner too fast, and the boy fell out. A buggy wheel ran over his head and made a deep cut in his scalp. Bleeding from the wound and suffering from shock, the young child somehow managed to get back on his feet and run after the buggy until his mother was able to stop the horse. He nearly bled to death before he reached the nearest hospital, twenty-five miles away.

In a sense, the political career of Richard "Dick" Nixon was marked again and again by this same pattern of falling from a lofty position and then staging an almost impossible comeback. Even after he left the presidency, scorned by many Americans for having brought shame to the highest office in the land, he refused to give up the fight. Slowly, painstakingly—and with some success—in his last years he worked to restore his image as a wise political counselor whose beliefs were expressed in books and speeches and whose advice was sought by later presidents.

Dick was born on January 9, 1913, in a small frame house that his father, Frank Nixon, had built in Yorba Linda, a small town in Southern California. Dick's mother, Hannah Milhous Nixon, was a devout Quaker who belonged to the Society of Friends Church. Quakers generally were hard-working people who lived according to a stern set of beliefs. They refused to fight in wars and were against all forms of human injustice, alcoholic drinks, using profanity, and even dancing.

Dick was the second son born to Hannah and Frank Nixon. Except for one son named for his father, the other Nixon boys all were named for early kings of England: Harold, Richard the Lion-Hearted, Arthur, and Edward. Two of these sons, Arthur and Harold, died at a young age.

The Nixons owned a small lemon grove in Yorba Linda, but it did not provide much income and they lived on the edge of poverty. Frank Nixon had to work at other jobs, including carpentry and ditch digging, to earn enough money to feed his large family. Since there were not enough funds to buy much new clothing, the older boys handed down their outgrown clothes to their younger brothers.

In 1922, when Dick was nine, the Nixons sold the lemon grove and moved to Whittier, fifteen miles from Los Angeles. Frank borrowed some money, bought a parcel of land along the road connecting the small towns of Whittier and La Habra, and opened a gas station. Later he added a small market next to the gas station.

When Dick was twelve, his younger brother Arthur died, and he was shattered by this family tragedy. "For weeks after Arthur's death," he later said, "there was not a day that I did not think about him and cry."[1] After this sad experience Dick was determined to try to make up for the loss of Arthur by becoming a success and making his parents proud of him.

Frank Nixon had been forced to drop out of school after the sixth grade because he needed to support himself, but he impressed upon his sons the importance of getting a good education. Dick took his father's advice to heart. He later remembered, "My biggest thrill in those years was to see the light in his eyes when I brought home a good report card."[2]

By nature, young Nixon was shy and reserved. He was a loner who found it painfully difficult to make friends in whom he could confide. But by his junior year at Whittier High School, he had decided to study law and hoped to become a politician. Dick realized that successful politicians need to be known and respected by a large number of people. This may have been one reason why he joined the school debate team and the Latin club, wrote for the school newspaper, participated in sports, performed in school plays, and played both the piano and the violin in musical productions.

Dick's life was not easy. In addition to studying hard for good grades and taking part in many extracurricular activities, he had to get up at four o'clock every morning and drive to Los Angeles to buy fresh fruit and vegetables for the family market. And he worked at the market nearly every weekend.

In his senior year, Dick won the Harvard Club of Southern California's award for the "best all-around student" and was offered a scholarship that would have paid part of his expenses at Harvard University. But that was in 1930—in the midst of the Great Depression—and his parents could not afford to send him to an expensive college far away from home. "My folks needed me," Dick explained. "They needed me in the store. There was no way I could go."[3]

Instead, Nixon went to nearby Whittier College. He continued to earn excellent grades and took part in many school activities. He became the college's champion debater, but in football he failed to make the first team, even after four seasons of hard-hitting practices. His coach worried about the physical beating that Dick took on the football field: "When he scrimmaged he was the cannon fodder. I used to get concerned at how we worked him over."[4]

After serving as student body president during his senior year, Dick graduated second in his class from Whittier College. Then he applied to various law schools. Duke University Law School in North Carolina gave him a scholarship that paid his full tuition, but he took part-time jobs because he had to pay for his housing and food. With three other students, he shared a one-room shack that had no plumbing or electricity. He shaved in the men's room in the library.

In 1937, Dick graduated third in his class at the law school. Returning home, he passed the California bar examination and became a lawyer. Then he found a job with a respected Whittier law firm.

The youthful attorney continued his interest in acting in amateur productions. One night he tried out for a part in a play called *The Dark Tower*, which was being staged by the Whittier Community Players. A woman auditioning for a leading role in this play was Thelma Catherine "Pat" Ryan, a typing and shorthand teacher at Whittier High School. She had strikingly attractive features and a cascade of golden-red hair.

Dick fell in love with her at first sight. When the try-outs finished (they both won parts in the play), Dick astounded Pat by saying to her, "You may not believe this but I am going to marry you someday."[5]

Like Dick, Pat had not enjoyed an easy or comfortable childhood. She was born in Ely, Nevada, the daughter of a struggling copper miner, and was nicknamed Pat because her birth date of March 16, 1912, fell on the eve of St. Patrick's Day. Her mother died when she was thirteen and her father when she was seventeen. Needing to support herself, she worked first as a secretary, then as an X-ray technician. She saved as much of her wages as possible, enrolled as a business major at the University of Southern California, and graduated with honors in 1937. Pat continued to work part-time in a variety of jobs, including that of a movie extra in such films as *Becky Sharp* and *The Great Ziegfeld*.

After dating for two years, Pat and Dick were married in 1940. They had two daughters, Patricia "Tricia" and Julie. In 1968, less than a month before her father became president, Julie married David Eisenhower, the grandson of President Eisenhower. Three years later Tricia married Edward Cox in a White House ceremony.

The United States was drawn into World War II after the Japanese bombed Pearl Harbor in December 1941. Despite the opposition of his Quaker religion to taking part in wars, Nixon wanted to help his country and joined the U.S. Navy as a lieutenant. He served in a unit in the South

Pacific that was responsible for getting supplies to the troops and removing wounded soldiers. His unit was bombed in the Solomon Islands twenty-eight nights out of thirty.

After the war Nixon entered the political arena in 1946 by winning the Republican nomination in his Whittier district for a seat in the House of Representatives. His opponent was Democrat Jerry Voorhis, who had held the office for five terms. At the time of this election, the Cold War between the Communists and the free world was beginning: Soviet Communists were threatening to expand their rule to other countries; stories of Communist spies appeared in the newspapers; fearful people worried that there might be Communist agents or sympathizers in the American government.

In his first political race, Nixon displayed a side to his character that was ruthless, underhanded, and at times dishonest. He falsely implied that Voorhis had Communist ties and said in one of his political ads that Voorhis's "voting record in Congress is more socialistic and communistic than Democratic."[6] This practice of smearing his opponent became a Nixon trademark that was repeated in later elections.

Nixon won the election and later told one of Voorhis's supporters, "Of course I knew Jerry Voorhis was not a communist, but I had to win. That's the thing you don't understand. The important thing is to win."[7]

Congressman Nixon first drew national attention after he became chairman of the House Un-American Activities Special Subcommittee. It investigated charges by Whittaker Chambers, a former Communist, who said that certain U.S. government officials had operated as

Communist spies in the past. Among those accused was Alger Hiss, who had held a high position in the State Department during World War II.

At first Hiss said that he had never met Chambers, but later he admitted that he knew him slightly under a different name. Hiss still denied, however, that he had ever been a Communist. Chambers then produced secret State Department documents—some in Hiss's handwriting—that he said Hiss had given to him. Some of these documents became known as the "pumpkin papers" because they were on microfilm that Chambers had hidden in a hollowed-out pumpkin on his farm. This evidence seemed to prove that Alger Hiss had been both a Communist and a spy.

Hiss was tried for perjury (lying under oath) and sentenced to prison. "The Hiss trial," Nixon later wrote, "for the first time, forcibly demonstrated to the American people that domestic Communism was a real and present danger to the security of the nation."[8]

In 1950, Nixon defeated Democrat Helen Gahagan Douglas in an election for a Senate seat. During the campaign he claimed that Douglas had Communist ties. He called her the Pink Lady and printed ads attacking her voting record on pink paper. (At that time the colors red and pink were often used to designate Communists.)

The rise of Nixon's political career was both swift and spectacular. At the age of thirty-seven he was the youngest member of the Senate. Two years later, he was selected to be the Republican nominee for the vice presidency on a ticket headed by General Dwight D. Eisenhower.

Shortly after he won the vice presidential nomination, Nixon was confronted by a charge that nearly ended his political career. Newspapers reported that he had a secret fund into which his friends and supporters had contributed about $18,000 by July 1952. Many outraged Americans, both Republicans and Democrats, insisted that if Nixon used this fund for his personal expenses, he should not run for the vice presidency.

To answer this charge, the California senator risked his entire political future on an emotional speech that was televised to the nation. He explained that none of the fund was spent for his personal use; it paid, instead, for political expenses that he felt should not be charged to the taxpayers. Then he listed his assets to prove he was not a wealthy man. Tearfully he related that some supporter had sent him a cocker spaniel that his daughter named Checkers. "The kids love that dog," he declared, "and I just want to say right now . . . we're going to keep it."[9]

He closed his "Checkers speech"—the first major political address on television—by suggesting that viewers send telegrams indicating whether they felt he should give up his place on the Republican ticket. An avalanche of telegrams supporting Nixon poured into the Republican National Headquarters, and Eisenhower agreed that Nixon should be kept as his running mate.

The Republicans won a resounding victory at the polls, and Richard Nixon, just a few days after his fortieth birthday, became the second-youngest vice president in history. He was active in this position, traveling to fifty-eight countries on official missions. And he kept the reins of government operating smoothly during the long period when President Eisenhower was recovering from the heart attack he suffered in 1955.

The Republican ticket of Eisenhower and Nixon was easily reelected in 1956. During the last part of his second term as vice president, Nixon began making plans to run for president in 1960. He won the Republican nomination, and his Democratic opponent was popular Senator John F. Kennedy of Massachusetts.

The 1960 campaign included the first presidential debates on television. In the first of four debates, Kennedy appeared more poised, self-confident, and vigorous than his rival. Nixon seemed nervous, hesitant, and tired.

The election results were extremely close. More than 68 million Americans cast ballots, and Kennedy barely captured the popular vote with 49.72 percent to Nixon's 49.55 percent. Kennedy's margin of victory in the electoral vote was 303 to 219, but if Nixon had won Illinois and Texas—which he lost by razor-thin margins—he would have become president.

Two years later, Nixon ran for governor of California against Democrat Edmund "Pat" Brown. When Brown defeated the former vice president, it appeared that Nixon's political career had ended. Bitterly he told reporters, "You won't have Nixon to kick around anymore, because, gentlemen, this is my last press conference."[10]

Nixon moved to New York City and practiced law. But he refused to retire from the political ring. During both the 1964 and 1966 elections he crisscrossed the country, delivering speeches at rallies for hundreds of Republican candidates.

In 1968, Nixon felt ready to attempt the most remarkable political comeback in history—to run for the presidency again. At this time there was enormous turmoil and unrest throughout the country. The Vietnam War was still raging, and there were huge, often bloody demonstrations urging the American government to withdraw its armed forces from this conflict in faraway Southeast Asia. Two of the most respected American leaders, civil rights activist Martin Luther King Jr. and antiwar Senator Robert F. Kennedy of New York, were both slain in 1968. And in many cities there were violent race riots that killed or injured many people and destroyed much property.

Nixon won the Republican nomination for the presidency, and Governor Spiro T. Agnew of Maryland was selected as the vice presidential candidate. The Democrats gave their presidential nomination to Vice President Hubert Humphrey, who previously had been a liberal senator from Minnesota. There was a powerful third-party candidate in this election—Alabama Governor George Wallace, who called for "law and order" and opposed civil rights measures intended to advance the integration of African-Americans.

In his campaign, Nixon also vowed to restore "law and order," and he promised to bring about "peace with honor" in Vietnam. He appealed to what he called the "Silent Majority," who eagerly looked forward to the end of strife and bloodshed in their streets and stopping the American casualties in Vietnam.

The 1968 election was almost as close as the 1960 election had been, but this time Nixon was victorious. He had 43.4 percent of the popular vote to Humphrey's 42.7 percent and Wallace's 13.5 percent.

There were some notable domestic achievements during the administration of President Nixon. To promote "law and order," Congress passed major crime bills that authorized more severe penalties for the most dangerous criminals and for those involved in selling drugs. The Nixon administration also adopted a program of revenue sharing that sent billions of dollars of federal taxes to state and local governments.

Several steps were taken during the Nixon presidency to improve the environment. The Environmental Protection Agency was set up to reduce pollution. Acts were passed to encourage recycling, restrict auto emissions, and curb the pollution of the nation's waterways from industrial waste materials.

While Nixon was in the White House, astronauts Neil Armstrong and Edwin Aldrin became the first men to walk on the moon, four days after the launching of *Apollo 11*. The overjoyed president proclaimed, "This is the greatest week in the history of the world since creation."[11]

The president announced that he would gradually withdraw American forces from Vietnam. He planned to turn over more of the fighting there to the South Vietnamese, who were battling Communist North Vietnam and its allies inside South Vietnam, known as the Vietcong. More than half a million Americans were stationed in Vietnam in 1969. By 1972, this number had been reduced to about twenty-five thousand.

But, while Nixon was gradually bringing more Americans home from the Asian battlefields, at the same time he was ordering massive bombing attacks on North Vietnamese cities and the mining of their harbors. Furthermore, in 1970, he directed American and South Vietnamese troops to invade Cambodia, South Vietnam's neighbor, in an effort to capture North Vietnamese soldiers stationed there and their supplies. This invasion led to a firestorm of protest in the United States, and it was soon ended.

A peace treaty was signed in January 1973, calling for

a halt to the warfare and the removal of the last U.S. forces from Vietnam. But fighting between the two Vietnams soon broke out again. North Vietnam conquered South Vietnam, destroyed its government, and united all the Vietnamese people under the Communist flag.

One of President Nixon's most important achievements involved opening the door to China. In 1949, China had fallen under the control of Communist leaders. For more than two decades, the United States had denied official recognition to the Communist Chinese government and blocked its admission to the United Nations. As a senator and later vice president, Nixon had been in the forefront of those who vigorously opposed any American ties to Red China.

After he became president, Nixon decided that the time had come to reverse the United States' position toward the Asian country with the world's largest population. In February 1972, he embarked on an eight-day visit to China in an effort to lay the groundwork for establishing normal relations with that country. His trip was televised, and for the first time millions of Americans had the opportunity to see what life was like in the giant nation they had been forbidden to enter.

The president's visit to China produced successful results. "We entered into agreements to expand cultural, educational, and journalistic contacts between our two countries," Nixon proudly proclaimed.[12] Later, the United States established full diplomatic relations with China and ended its opposition to China's entering the United Nations.

Just as President Nixon had lessened tensions with China, he also was determined to provide better relations with the other bastion of communism, the Soviet Union. In

May 1972, he and Soviet leader Leonid Brezhnev signed the first arms-control agreements placing sharp restrictions on nuclear weapons. Both countries agreed to limit their antiballistic missile sites and freeze the number of strategic offensive ballistic missiles at current levels. These agreements provided the first steps toward ending the Cold War that had existed since the conclusion of World War II.

In 1972, President Nixon and Vice President Agnew were reelected in one of the largest landslides in political history. Only one state, Massachusetts, and the District of Columbia were won by the Democratic presidential candidate, Senator George McGovern of South Dakota. Yet neither Nixon nor Agnew served even two years of their second terms.

Agnew was accused of accepting bribes while serving as governor of Maryland and later, as vice president. He resigned from office in 1973. Under the provisions of the Twenty-fifth Amendment, President Nixon then appointed House Minority Leader Gerald R. Ford as the new vice president.

Nixon's second term in the White House was shortened by the Watergate affair—the worst scandal in any presidential administration. It began on June 17, 1972, when five agents of the president's reelection committee were arrested while burglarizing and planting bugs in the office of the Democratic National Headquarters, located in a complex of buildings known as the Watergate.

The sordid Watergate story is long and complicated, but basically, a series of investigations revealed that crimes had been committed by many of the highest officials in the Nixon administration. These officials included cabinet members and the president's closest advisers.

Even more serious, the president himself was involved in trying to cover up the Watergate scandal. He had obstructed justice by such acts as approving the payment of hush money to the Watergate burglars and by ordering the Central Intelligence Agency (CIA) to suspend the investigation of misdeeds that was being conducted by the Federal Bureau of Investigation (FBI). Among the other accusations leveled at Nixon were abusing the powers of his office, withholding evidence, making false statements to investigators, and encouraging government officials to lie.

The House of Representatives drew up impeachment charges to remove Nixon from the presidency. He then would have been tried by the Senate, and if found guilty, he would have been stripped of his office. But rather than being forced out of the White House, on August 9, 1974, Richard Nixon became the first chief executive to resign from the presidency.

Many of Nixon's aides went to jail for the roles they had played in the Watergate affair. Some Americans felt that the fallen president also should have been tried in court for his alleged crimes. However, one month after Nixon stepped down from office President Ford granted him a pardon for any or all offenses he may have committed during his presidential administration. Ford insisted that the humiliation of resigning the presidency in disgrace was sufficient punishment and equal to "serving a jail term."[13]

For several years after he left Washington, D.C., Nixon remained in seclusion. He wrote nine books—some were memoirs and others dealt with government issues, especially foreign affairs. Beginning in 1978, Nixon started playing a public role again. He visited many countries, made speeches, and conferred with leaders at home and abroad. Shortly before his death on April 22, 1994, at the age of eighty-one, he traveled to Russia and reported his observations to President Bill Clinton.

The former president tried in his later years to regain some measure of respect as a well-informed elder statesman. But he never could escape the dark shadow that had fallen over his once brilliant career. "The way I tried to deal with Watergate," he said in 1974, "is a burden that I shall bear for every day of the life that is left to me."[14]

2

JIMMY CARTER

As a child, James Earl Carter Jr. was called Jimmy. When he became an adult, he continued to be known by this nickname. Even after he became president, the congressional bills and treaties that required his signature always bore the name of Jimmy Carter.

Jimmy was born in the small town of Plains, Georgia, on October 1, 1924. He was the oldest of four children. His father, James Earl Carter Sr., was a farmer who raised cotton, corn, and peanuts. He also founded a peanut warehouse in Plains, where other nearby peanut farmers brought their crops. Always interested in politics, Jimmy's father was elected to the Georgia legislature in 1952 but died the following year.

Lillian Gordy Carter, Jimmy's mother, was a remarkable woman. Besides all her household duties, she worked as a nurse and cared for both white and black patients. This was at a time when racial segregation was still entrenched in the South, and her white neighbors criticized her for tending to the medical needs of African-Americans. But Miss Lillian, as she was called, strongly believed in racial equality and refused to be swayed by the opinions of prejudiced people.

In 1966 at the age of sixty-eight, Miss Lillian volunteered for the Peace Corps. After studying the Marathi language, she was sent to India. There she spent two years, providing birth control information to many poor people who lived in one of the world's most overpopulated countries.

Jimmy Carter grew up in a family that was fairly prosperous, but the Carters did not enjoy many of the comforts that we take for granted today. As a young child, Jimmy lived in a house that had no electricity or running water. The bathroom was in the backyard, water was provided by a pump outdoors, the house was heated only by fireplaces, and Miss Lillian cooked on a wood-burning stove.

Young Jimmy had tasks to perform every morning before he went to school. The farm bell rang at 4 A.M., and a short time later Jimmy joined his father at the barn. By lantern light they harnessed mules to a wagon and set off to the red clay fields. When Jimmy was small, he carried water and ran errands for the hired farm workers. As he grew older, he learned how to help plow the land, plant the cotton, corn, and peanuts, and harvest the crops.

After school and on weekends, Jimmy had regular chores that included feeding livestock, pumping and hauling water, and chopping wood for the fireplaces and stove. One chore that he hated was "mopping" cotton. First he put into a bucket a mixture of molasses, arsenic, and water. Then, dipping a small rag mop into the bucket, he had to daub its sticky contents onto each bud of cotton.

The job was messy and exhausting, but it was necessary to get rid of the boll weevils (insects) that would kill the cotton. Swarms of flies, attracted to the molasses, would bite Jimmy's arms and face. By the end of the day, his pants would be covered with the syrupy mess. When he took off his jeans, he stood them up in his bedroom because they were too stiff to bend.

Most of the other children in the neighborhood were African-Americans. "When I was a boy," Jimmy wrote many years later, "almost all my playmates were black. We worked in the fields together, and hunted and fished and swam together, but when it was time for church or for school we went our separate ways, without really under-standing why. Our lives were dominated by unspoken, unwritten, but powerful rules, rules that were almost never challenged."[1]

The schools in Plains were not large or furnished with the best equipment, but Jimmy was a very good student and became interested in many subjects. He learned how to debate, memorize poems, read music, and solve arith-metic problems.

His favorite subject was reading. When friends and relatives asked him what presents he wanted for Christmas or his birthday, he replied, "Books!" One day he announced joyfully, "Mama, I don't *ever* want to stop learning."[2]

The Carter family was not wealthy enough to finance a four-year college education for Jimmy. So he decided at an early age that he wanted to attend the U.S. Naval Academy at Annapolis, Maryland. There he could receive an excellent, government-paid education and become a naval officer.

After graduating from high school at the age of six-teen, Jimmy enrolled at Georgia Southwestern College to take a chemistry course that the Naval Academy required. Then, while waiting to learn whether the academy had accepted him, he took math courses at Georgia Tech.

Finally, Jimmy received the good news that he had qualified to study at the academy. He enrolled there in 1943, at a time when the United States was in the midst of fighting in World War II. Because of the urgent need for more naval officers, Jimmy was able to complete his studies in three years and graduated in the top tenth of his class in 1946.

Jimmy's best subjects were electronics, gunnery, and naval tactics. At the academy he also learned how to fly airplanes. His athletic activities included running in cross-country races and track meets, and he enjoyed playing football on the "skinny" team made up of men who all weighed under one hundred and forty pounds.

Home on leave from Annapolis in the summer of 1945, Jimmy's attention was drawn to Rosalynn Smith, a seventeen-year-old who was the best friend of his sister Ruth. She lived in Plains and worked after school in the local beauty parlor and as a seamstress to help her widowed mother meet expenses. A bright high-school student, she later studied interior decorating at Georgia Southwestern College.

Rosalynn had visited the Carter home many times, but Jimmy had paid little attention to her because she was three years younger than he was. However, Rosalynn had thought often of him, and she was thrilled when he asked her to go to a movie with him. "After dreaming about him for so long," she said, "I was actually with him, and it couldn't have been more wonderful. . . . I was completely swept off my feet."[3] Later Rosalynn learned Jimmy had told his mother after that first date "that he was going to marry me someday."[4]

On July 7, 1946, a month after his graduation, Ensign Jimmy Carter married Rosalynn Smith in Plains. They had four children: John William "Jack" in 1947, James Earl III "Chip" in 1950, Donnell Jeffrey "Jeff" in 1952, and—much later—Amy Lynn in 1967.

Rosalynn enjoyed her life as a naval officer's wife, even though her husband was often away from home on sea duty. In the years that followed his naval career, Rosalynn helped her husband by working as the bookkeeper for the Carter peanut business, campaigning for him in his elections, undertaking diplomatic missions for him as president, and serving as his trusted adviser.

During his first two years in the navy, Carter was an electronics instructor aboard the battleships *Wyoming* and *Mississippi*. In 1948, he was accepted for submarine duty and attended the submarine school in New London, Connecticut, for six months.

His first submarine assignment was aboard the *Pomfret*, which set out from Hawaii for the Far East. During that trip the future president nearly lost his life. The sub had to surface each night to recharge its batteries. One night when the sub was surfacing and a torrential storm was raging, Jimmy was standing watch on the sub's bridge and holding tightly to the handrail.

Suddenly a towering wave rose about six feet over his head. The driving force of the water tore Jimmy's hands from the rail. It swept him off the bridge and carried him about thirty feet back along the deck. He tried to swim but could only thrash his arms around helplessly. Finally he crashed into the barrel of a large mounted cannon and hung onto it with all his might until the water receded. Had the sub been tilted in a slightly different direction, he would have been swept overboard.

When the U.S. Navy began to build nuclear-powered

submarines, Carter was eager to serve on one of these new ships. The first two atomic subs were to be called the *Nautilus* and the *Sea Wolf*. They were constructed under the guidance of Admiral Hyman Rickover, who had convinced the government that submarines powered by nuclear energy were vital to the success of future naval operations.

In 1952, Carter was sent to a New York State college to take advanced courses in nuclear physics. But before the navy could assign him as an officer on one of the new subs, he first had to be approved by Admiral Rickover. Near the end of a grueling two-hour interview, Rickover asked Lieutenant Carter how high he had ranked in his class at the Naval Academy. Jimmy proudly replied that he had ranked fifty-ninth in a class of 820 midshipmen.

Rickover stared intently at Carter and then asked, "Did you do your best?"

Remembering the times when he could have studied harder than he did, Carter nervously confessed, "No, sir, I didn't always do my best."

The admiral shifted uneasily in his chair and abruptly inquired, "Why not?"[5] Then he said no more and the interview ended.

Even though Jimmy felt discouraged after the interview, he was chosen by Rickover to serve as the engineering officer aboard the *Sea Wolf*. However, the admiral's final words left a lasting impression on the twenty-eight-year-old sailor. Many years later, in 1976, his campaign autobiography was titled *Why Not the Best?*

After his father died in 1953, Jimmy faced a difficult decision. Should he continue his successful naval career or return to Plains and take over the operation of his family's farm and peanut warehouse business? Although Rosalynn wanted him to stay in the navy, Jimmy resigned his commission and moved back to Plains. "I had only one life to live," he explained, "and I wanted to live it as a civilian, with a potentially fuller opportunity for varied public service."6

Gradually, with the help of Rosalynn, he expanded the family business into a thriving enterprise. Modern farming techniques enabled his peanut production to increase steadily, and his warehouse prospered as he convinced more peanut farmers to bring him their crops.

Soon he became active in local civic and church affairs. He served for seven years on the Sumter County Board of Education and played a role in organizations that worked to improve living conditions in his region. After the 1954 Supreme Court decision outlawing segregation in the public schools aroused bitter opposition in the South, Carter emerged as a voice of reason calling for racial equality. Alone among the business owners in Plains, he refused to join the White Citizens' Council that was established to fight the Court order to integrate schools.

A deeply religious man, Carter read the Bible daily, faithfully attended the Baptist Church, and taught both Sunday school and adult Bible classes. When his church's congregation voted to keep African-Americans out of worship services, six persons voted to admit them—five Carters and one neighbor.

In 1962, Carter ran for a seat in the Georgia State Senate. On the day of the primary election it appeared that his opponent had eked out a narrow victory for the Democratic nomination. But Carter was able to prove that vote fraud had taken place and that some votes counted for his rival had been "cast" by dead people and prisoners. So Carter was certified as the Democratic nominee and easily defeated the Republican candidate in the general election.

The peanut farmer-turned-politician was shocked to discover how powerful the lobbyists and special interest groups were in getting their bills passed. He strongly felt that citizens deserved more lawmakers responsible to the ordinary people, not to the rich and privileged.

Carter was reelected to the state senate and then ran for governor in 1966. He was defeated but tried again in 1970, and this time was victorious.

In his inaugural address, Governor Carter told his fellow Georgians, "I say to you quite frankly that the time for racial discrimination is over."[7] The new governor appointed many blacks to previously all-white boards and agencies and increased the number of black state employees by 40 percent. He also placed the portrait of slain civil rights leader Martin Luther King Jr. in the state capitol.

Governor Carter reorganized the state government, abolishing many departments and agencies by combining their functions and services. This resulted in substantial savings and provided the Georgia state treasury with a $200 million surplus.

In Georgia, at that time, governors could not run for reelection, so Carter found himself without a political job when his term ended in 1975. But he soon plunged into the nation's most important political sweepstakes—the presidential race. When he announced his plan to seek the presidency, many people believed that Carter, scarcely known outside his own state, must have been joking. His mother, however, thought differently. "I could tell by his face he wasn't kidding," she said. "When he says he is going to do something, he usually does."[8]

At the beginning of the 1976 presidential campaign, most voters had never heard of the ambitious peanut farmer. "Jimmy who?" they asked. To become better known, Carter traveled across the country many times, shaking thousands of strangers' hands, and saying, "My name is Jimmy Carter, and I'm running for president."[9]

Once they knew more about him, many Democrats cast their ballots for Carter in state primary elections. By the time the Democratic National Convention met in July, he had enough delegates pledged to him to give him the nomination. The convention selected Senator Walter Mondale of Minnesota as his vice presidential running mate.

To run against Carter, the Republicans nominated President Gerald Ford, who had been elevated from the vice presidency to the presidency following the resignation of Richard Nixon in 1974. Ford's running mate was Senator Bob Dole of Kansas.

The election was hotly contested, and the results were close. Carter's winning margin in the popular vote was 50.1 percent to Ford's 48.0 percent. The electoral vote was 297 for Carter and 240 for Ford.

Why had a virtually unknown candidate from the Deep South (which had not produced a president since Zachary Taylor in 1848) been able to win the White House without ever holding an office in Washington, D.C.? At the time of the 1976 election, the sordid Watergate affair still hung like a dark cloud over the nation. The voters turned to Carter largely because he was an *outsider* who had no connection with the mess in Washington. And they believed him when he pledged in his inaugural address "to stay close to you, to be worthy of you, and to exemplify what you are."[10]

To demonstrate his closeness to the people, immediately after the inaugural ceremonies, President Carter left his bullet-proof limousine—together with Rosalynn and daughter Amy—to walk the mile-and-a-half parade route from the Capitol to the White House.

In his first full day in office, Carter pardoned the estimated ten thousand young men who had evaded the draft during the Vietnam War. He hoped that such action would help the American people put behind them the ugly scars created by that war.

While being an outsider who had just arrived in Washington, D.C., gave Carter the advantage of not being associated with the Watergate scandal, it gave him a disadvantage, too. The new president had no experience with the way business operated in the nation's capital and no close friends in Congress on whom he could rely for support and advice. So on various issues, a tug-of-war developed between the inexperienced president and the lawmakers on Capitol Hill.

The energy program that the president proposed soon after taking office illustrated his problems with Congress. Carter asserted that the United States faced the possibility of a "national catastrophe" unless the people gave up their wasteful use of energy and adopted a program that would be "the moral equivalent of war."[11] He called on Congress to provide a wide range of energy measures, which included a 50¢-per-gallon tax on gasoline, searching for new oil and gas supplies, developing synthetic fuels, requiring industry to convert from oil to coal as its chief source of power, and creating a Department of Energy.

Except for establishing the new Department of Energy, Congress dragged its heels on most of Carter's energy proposals. Finally, in 1978 and 1980, the lawmakers passed some watered-down energy measures that were short of what the president had wanted.

The cornerstone of President Carter's foreign policy was a strong demand that human rights must be observed throughout the world. He lashed out at the Soviet government for its harsh treatment of Russian writers who had dared to speak out against the oppressive Communist rule. "But such violations," he said, "are not limited to one country or one ideology. There are other countries that violate human rights in one way or another—by torture, by political persecution, and by racial or religious discrimination."[12]

Another issue that concerned Carter was the growing resentment felt by the people of Panama because the United States controlled both the Panama Canal and the Canal Zone in which it was located. Long before, in 1903, Panama had agreed by treaty to let the United States use and control part of its land for the purpose of building and operating a canal that would link the Atlantic and Pacific Oceans. As the years passed, however, angry Panamanians cried out for the return of their land and the right to receive the tolls paid by shippers who used the canal.

President Carter labored with Panamanian officials to create a new treaty that would settle this problem. He faced stiff opposition from many Americans who claimed that the canal must not be "given away," but he refused to cave in to his opponents. "I believed that a new treaty was necessary," Carter wrote in his memoirs. "I was convinced that we needed to correct an injustice."[13]

The treaty had to be ratified by two-thirds of the Senate, and the president waged a vigorous campaign to convince senators to vote in its favor. It was ratified by only one more vote than the two-thirds minimum. The treaty provided that the Canal Zone territory would be turned over to the Panamanians immediately and that they would assume full control of the canal on December 31, 1999. (A second treaty reserved the right of the United States to intervene with military force if the canal's security ever was threatened.)

Carter's most brilliant personal achievement came in 1978 when he undertook the nearly impossible task of ending the long-existing state of war between Israel and Egypt. To work on resolving the disputes between their two countries, Carter invited Prime Minister Menachem Begin of Israel and President Anwar Sadat of Egypt to meet at Camp David, the presidential retreat in Maryland.

During thirteen days of intense negotiations, with Carter acting as the conciliator friendly to both sides, Begin and Sadat found major points on which they could agree. At the end of the negotiations, they signed agreements that provided the framework for a peace treaty that followed.

In 1979, after seven years of negotiations that had begun under President Nixon, American and Soviet diplomats agreed on a new strategic arms limitation treaty called SALT II. President Carter urged the Senate to ratify this treaty, declaring that reducing the number of strategic missile systems would reduce the threat of nuclear war. But before the Senate could act on this treaty, the Soviets invaded neighboring Afghanistan, which infuriated Carter and many other world leaders.

The American president asserted that the Soviet invasion of Afghanistan was "the gravest threat to peace" since 1945.[14] Striking back at the Soviets, he asked the Senate to end its consideration of SALT II. He shut off the sales of grain and high-tech products to the Soviet Union. Also, he persuaded the United States Olympic Committee not to send an American team to the 1980 Olympic Games to be held in Moscow.

On November 4, 1979, members of a militant group that had seized control of Iran stormed the U.S. embassy in Teheran, the capital of Iran, and took more than sixty Americans hostage. The Iranian extremists took this action because the shah (ruler) they had overthrown had been allowed to enter the United States for medical treatment. A few of the American hostages were freed within three weeks, but the remaining fifty-two Americans were held captive for more than a year.

President Carter worked strenuously to free the Americans. All efforts to gain their release through negotiations failed. He suspended oil imports from Iran and blocked the Iranians from removing their investments and other assets they owned in the United States. In a desperate move, he ordered a small American military force to attempt a secret rescue of the captives. But this effort was unsuccessful and resulted in the deaths of eight marines.

At the time of the 1980 presidential election, many

Americans claimed Carter was weak and ineffective because he had been unable to bring the hostages home. Adding to his unpopularity with the public, rising unemployment gripped the nation, and runaway inflation forced consumers to pay higher prices for products. Many people were angered because they could not afford the products they needed.

Carter's Republican opponent in 1980 was popular Ronald Reagan, the former governor of California. Reagan easily defeated Carter, who carried only six states. Ironically, on January 20, 1981—the day Reagan was inaugurated as president—the Iranian government finally released the American hostages.

Jimmy Carter has become a very active former president. He and Rosalynn are both involved in Habitat for Humanity, a nonprofit organization that builds houses for needy people in the United States and other countries. Often the Carters don their jeans and wield hammers and saws to help construct homes for the homeless.

The former president and his wife created and operate the Carter Center in Atlanta, Georgia. Here, they labor to help reduce disease, homelessness, and conflict throughout the world. Among the center's many achievements are the reduction of river blindness, a condition that affects millions of citizens in underdeveloped countries, and the near-extinction of Guinea worm disease, which once infected two million people a year in parts of Africa and India.

Carter also has served as a diplomatic envoy who attempts to reduce tensions in many parts of the world. In the year 1994, he persuaded North Korea to modify its potentially dangerous nuclear program, negotiated a last-minute agreement that spared Haiti from a military invasion, and patched together a temporary truce between warring groups in Bosnia.

When Carter was asked why he and his wife spend so much of their time trying to help others, he smiled and replied, "We do what makes us happy."[15]

3

RONALD REAGAN

When Ronald Reagan was elected to the presidency in 1980, he became involved in one of the strangest and most persistent jinxes in political history. Every president since 1840 who had been elected in a zero year, such as 1900 or 1920, had died in office.

On March 30, 1981, scarcely two months after he had moved into the White House, Reagan was the target of an insane assassin. After making a speech at a hotel in Washington, D.C., the president was walking toward his limousine when John Hinckley Jr. drew his revolver and fired six shots. One of the bullets entered Reagan's left side, pierced a lung, and lodged just inches from his heart. Three other men were wounded, including the president's press secretary, James Brady, who was left partially paralyzed after a bullet penetrated his brain. (The Brady Act, passed by Congress in 1993 to restrict the sale of handguns, was named in honor of the president's aide.)

Reagan lost much blood and had to undergo two hours of surgery to remove the bullet and care for his wound. Following this delicate procedure, the amiable president jokingly said, "I forgot to duck."[1] He recovered completely from his close call with death. And when he left the White House at the end of two terms, the oldest president in history finally had broken the zero-year jinx.

Ronald Wilson Reagan was born on February 6, 1911, the second son of Jack and Nelle Wilson Reagan. He was a large baby, weighing ten pounds at birth. The first time Jack saw his bawling son he said, "For such a little bit of a fat Dutchman, he makes a lot of noise, doesn't he?"[2] Jack nicknamed him "Dutch," and for many years the future president was known by this nickname.

Dutch was born in the small town of Tampico, Illinois, but his family moved several times while he was young. His father was a shoe salesman, and he worked in various towns and cities. He seldom held a job very long, partly because of business conditions and partly because he was an alcoholic.

When Dutch was nine, the family settled permanently in Dixon, Illinois, about eighty miles west of Chicago. Jack Reagan borrowed enough money to become part owner of a shoe store, but it became a victim of the Depression and had to close. Nelle Reagan worked as a clerk and a seamstress in a dress shop to help increase the family's meager income.

Dutch enjoyed his boyhood years in Dixon. In high school he played right guard on the football team, made the basketball and track teams, was elected president of the student body, and acted in school plays. In the summers he worked as a lifeguard, watching over the crowds that swam in nearby Rock River on hot days. During a period of eight years he was credited with rescuing seventy-seven swimmers in danger of drowning.

Reagan attended Eureka College, a small Disciples of Christ school near Peoria, Illinois. He earned part of his college expenses washing dishes in his fraternity house and a girls' dormitory. He continued playing football and acting, joined the swimming and debate teams, and took an important part in college politics. His many college activities were more important to him than his studies, and his grades were only average.

After graduation in 1932, Reagan decided to become a radio sports announcer. Finding a job during the Depression was difficult, but he hitchhiked from station to station. Finally, the program director at WOC in Davenport, Iowa, hired him. He did well at this job and then moved to a larger station, WHO, in Des Moines, Iowa.

Young Reagan became widely known in the Midwest as the broadcaster of major league baseball games and Big Ten football games. But he did not attend these games in person. Instead, while sitting in the Des Moines radio studio, he had to rely on telegraph messages that were sent from the ballpark press box after each play. Then he had to use his imagination to describe these plays to his audience.

Once while Reagan was broadcasting an exciting Chicago Cubs game, the telegraph connection suddenly broke down. Augie Galan of the Cubs was at bat in the ninth inning. For a period of more than six minutes, Reagan had to relate an imaginary story of what was taking place at the ballpark. He said that Galan fouled numerous balls and described at length "a red headed kid who had scrambled and gotten the souvenir ball."[3] Finally the telegraph wire was restored, and Reagan returned to announcing the true facts about the game.

In 1937, the Cubs held their spring training practice in California, and Reagan accompanied the team. He visited some Hollywood motion picture studios, and a friend arranged a screen test for him.

The studio executives were favorably impressed by the twenty-six-year-old sportscaster. He read lines superbly and had a deep, resonant voice. Moreover, he was very handsome. Standing six feet, one inch tall, Reagan had the build of an athlete. He had thick, brown wavy hair, beautiful blue-gray eyes, and a warm, friendly smile.

Warner Brothers Studio signed him to a seven-year movie contract. That was the beginning of a film career that spanned more than a quarter of a century and led him to appear in fifty-three movies. He made his screen debut in *Love Is on the Air* (1937) and was cast in a role that he already knew—that of a radio announcer.

Many of his films were known as B pictures, low-budget movies that often were shown at theaters as second features that accompanied more expensive A pictures. He also made some major movies, such as *Knute Rockne, All American* (1940). In this film he was cast as George Gipp, a dying football player on Rockne's Notre Dame team. This movie gave rise to the emotion-charged plea, "Win one for the Gipper!"[4]

What is generally considered Reagan's finest performance occurred in *Kings Row* (1942), which was nominated for an Oscar as the best motion picture of the year. He portrayed a man whose legs were amputated by an insane doctor. When the unfortunate man discovered he had no legs, he cried out in horror, "Where's the rest of me?"[5] (This anguished cry was the title of a book that Reagan co-authored in 1965.)

Except for his final film, *The Killers* (1964), in which he played a villain, Reagan nearly always was cast as a wholesome, good-humored, likable person. This gained him widespread approval from millions of movie fans. The "good guy" image carried over into his political career and probably helped him win many votes at the polls.

In 1940, Reagan married film star Jane Wyman. They had a daughter, Maureen, and adopted a son, Michael. But their eight-year marriage ended in divorce.

World War II interrupted Reagan's acting career. He served in the U.S. Army, rising from second lieutenant to captain. Because of poor eyesight he was not assigned to combat duty. Instead, he was sent to a motion picture unit in which he narrated films to train bomber pilots and other military personnel.

Reagan married another Hollywood actress, Nancy Davis, in 1952. They had two children, Patricia "Patti" and Ronald "Ron" Prescott. The Reagans made one film together, *Hellcats of the Navy* (1957), and then Nancy retired from acting.

Ronald and Nancy Reagan were known as one of Hollywood's most devoted couples. "I've often said my life really began with Ronnie," Nancy explained, "and I think to a great extent it did. What I really wanted out of life was to be a wife to the man I loved and mother to our children."[6]

When Reagan's movie career began to decline, he turned to television. From 1954 to 1962 he hosted the *General Electric Theater* television series and sometimes acted in its dramatic stories. His duties also included touring the General Electric factories around the country and speaking to their employees. He talked about his Hollywood experiences and also discussed some of his political beliefs. Often Reagan said he was deeply concerned about "how the ever-expanding federal government was encroaching on liberties we'd always taken for granted."[7]

As a young man, Reagan had been a strong Democrat whose hero was Democratic President Franklin D. Roosevelt. For six years he served as president of the Screen Actors Guild, a labor organization representing thousands of actors. But as the years passed, he grew more conservative. In 1952, for the first time, he voted for a Republican presidential candidate, Dwight D. Eisenhower, and in 1960 he was active in the "Democrats for Nixon" campaign. A short time after this election he changed his voter registration from Democrat to Republican.

Reagan first achieved political prominence in 1964 when he delivered a stirring speech on behalf of Barry Goldwater, the very conservative Republican candidate for president. Although Goldwater lost the election, Reagan's fiery speech in opposition to big government and high taxes drew contributions totaling hundreds of thousands of dollars to the Republican campaign.

In 1966, Reagan's conservative friends urged him to run for governor of California, and he accepted the challenge. Many people scoffed at the chances of a politically inexperienced movie actor to defeat two-term Governor Edmund G. "Pat" Brown. But Reagan won the election easily and four years later was reelected.

After taking office as governor, Reagan ran the state government like the chairman of a large corporation. He stated his general beliefs and then encouraged department heads and other aides to turn these beliefs into policies.

Governor Reagan was concerned because the previous administration had run up debts of $194 million. So, even though he had campaigned against higher taxes, Reagan felt it was necessary to balance the budget and coaxed the legislature to increase income taxes. By the time that he left office, the state treasury had a surplus.

The governor's welfare reform plan cut many thousands of the less needy people from the rolls of those who received government payments. At the same time, however, welfare benefits were increased to those poor people who met stricter requirements.

Protests against the Vietnam War on the state's college campuses happened frequently while Reagan was governor. When rioting and destruction occurred on some campuses, Reagan quickly called upon state troops to stop the violence. "This administration," he warned, "will do whatever is possible to maintain order on our campuses. . . . I don't care what force it takes. That force must be applied."[8]

Reagan chose not to run for a third term as governor in 1974, but two years later he had his eye on the presidency. He challenged President Gerald R. Ford for the 1976 Republican presidential nomination. The Californian received strong support from conservatives and won many convention delegates from the South and West. But at the convention Ford eked out a narrow victory, gaining the votes of 1,187 delegates to 1,070 for Reagan. In the general election, Democrat Jimmy Carter defeated Ford and won the presidency.

Four years later, in 1980, Reagan tried again to capture the Republican presidential nomination, and this time he succeeded. His Democratic opponent was President Carter, and the challenger from California quickly took the offensive in the campaign.

Reagan blamed Carter for being unable to bring home the Americans held hostage by terrorists in Iran. He said the president had failed to deal effectively with inflation and unemployment. (During 1980, the inflation rate soared to 15 percent and more than 7 percent of the nation's workers had no jobs.) Reagan also charged that President Carter had allowed the Soviets to move dangerously ahead of the Americans in the crucial arms race. The Republican candidate often declared, "National defense is not a threat to peace; it is the guarantee of peace with freedom."[9]

On Election Day, voters sent the former movie actor to the White House. Reagan received 51 percent of the popular vote to Carter's 41 percent and 489 electoral votes to Carter's 49. A third presidential candidate, independent John B. Anderson, a former Republican congressman from Illinois, captured nearly 7 percent of the popular vote but no electoral votes because he carried no states.

To stimulate the economy, President Reagan proposed slashing income and corporate taxes. He believed that substantial tax cuts would increase economic activity so much that tax revenues would rise, not fall. Reagan also called upon Congress to make large budget cuts in nearly all areas except national defense, whose budget he felt must be increased. The president's economic policies came to be known as *Reaganomics*.

By August 1981, Congress had passed many of Reagan's economic proposals, including the largest income tax cut in American history. But in 1981 and 1982, the economy suffered a severe recession in which millions of people were thrown out of work and the productivity of industries declined sharply. Lower taxes and increased defense spending helped produce a growing federal deficit, or debt.

In 1982, Congress reversed its earlier position and

adopted higher income taxes. Economic conditions improved steadily in 1983 and generally remained prosperous during the rest of the Reagan administration. Many people, however, were dismayed by the rise of the national debt while Reagan was in office. During his eight-year presidency it nearly tripled, soaring from about $900 billion in 1980 to more than $2.68 trillion in 1988.

Reagan was daring in his moves to promote the cause of women in government. In 1981, he appointed the first woman justice to serve on the United States Supreme Court. She was Sandra Day O'Connor, an Arizona state appeals court judge. He was the first president to have three women serving in cabinet-level posts at the same time—Elizabeth H. Dole, secretary of transportation; Margaret M. Heckler, secretary of health and human services; and Jeane J. Kirkpatrick, U.S. representative to the United Nations.

In 1982, President Reagan sent eight hundred U.S. Marines to Beirut, Lebanon, to join an international peacekeeping force overseeing the withdrawal of Palestinian terrorists. Explosives set off by terrorists on October 23, 1983, destroyed the headquarters building of the U.S. forces, killing 241 marines. Unable to bring an end to the fighting in Lebanon, the United States and its allies withdrew their forces in 1984.

Just two days after the marines were killed in Beirut, attention shifted to the tiny Caribbean island nation of Grenada. Grenadian rebels, with close ties to Cuba's Communist dictator, Fidel Castro, had just overthrown their government. United States government officials said they feared for the safety of nearly six hundred American medical students enrolled at Grenada's school of medicine.

President Reagan ordered a military invasion of Grenada. American forces quickly defeated the Grenadian troops and about seven hundred Cubans on the island who fought the invaders. Nineteen Americans were killed and 116 were wounded in this brief military action.

As Reagan advanced through his first presidential term, he won the respect and affection of a large number of Americans. They admired his personal warmth, good humor, and constant optimism that their country's best days still lay ahead. They appreciated his determination to help solve the nation's problems and called him the "Great Communicator" because he spoke to them in straightforward, simple messages that were easily understood. Democratic House Speaker Thomas "Tip" O'Neill said, "There's something about the guy that people like. They want him to be a success."[10]

Reagan's popularity was confirmed in the 1984 presidential election when he ran for a second term. His Democratic opponent was Walter F. Mondale, who had served as vice president under Jimmy Carter. Mondale's vice presidential running mate was Congresswoman Geraldine Ferraro, the first woman nominated for this position by a major political party.

President Reagan and Vice President George Bush won in a landslide. They had 59 percent of the popular vote to 41 percent for the Mondale-Ferraro ticket. Mondale carried the single state of Minnesota and the District of Columbia. He won only 13 electoral votes compared to 525 for Reagan.

Even in his seventies, Reagan generally was in good health. He exercised daily in the White House, and when he vacationed at his ranch near Santa Barbara, California, he split wood for fences and chopped brush. And he rode horses as often as possible. One of his favorite quotations was, "There's nothing so good for the inside of a man as the outside of a horse."[11]

In July 1985, doctors discovered a cancerous tumor growing in the president's colon. Reagan then signed a statement temporarily delegating all presidential powers to Vice President Bush while he was undergoing surgery. The operation was successful, and the president recovered rapidly.

One of Reagan's most controversial proposals to Congress called for creating the Strategic Defense Initiative (SDI), or Star Wars, as it was called by its critics. The president hoped that SDI would be a space-based defense system capable of forming a high-tech defensive shield over Americans against incoming missiles. "If we can get a system which is effective," he told Congress, "we would be back in the situation we were in [after World War II], when we were the only nation with the nuclear weapon, and we did not threaten others with it."[12]

Critics of SDI argued that total security against enemy missiles could never be scientifically achieved. Moreover, SDI was an extremely expensive proposal, and although Congress approved a small fraction of the funds needed for its development, the project was never completed.

The Reagan administration lost some of its popularity because of the role that it played in an affair that involved both Nicaragua and Iran. In 1979, rebels known as Sandinistas overthrew the dictator of Nicaragua and set up a pro-Communist government. President Reagan sought to drive the Sandinistas from power by supporting non-

Communist warriors called the *contras* (Spanish for "against"). Congress voted in 1981 to send some weapons to the contras, but the fighting dragged on without either side gaining a decisive victory.

In 1984, fear that American military forces might become involved in the Nicaraguan civil war led Congress to adopt the Boland Amendment, forbidding further U.S. military aid to the contras. Officials in the Reagan administration, angered by this amendment, then sought indirect means of helping the contras.

Meanwhile, in another part of the world, Lebanese terrorists friendly to Iran were holding several Americans hostage. President Reagan authorized the secret sale of arms to Iran. Apparently he did this in hopes that Iran then would persuade the terrorists in Lebanon to release the American hostages. At that time, however, the United States had a policy that banned the sale of weapons to Iran and other countries thought to be supporters of terrorism. The secret arms deal led to the release of only three hostages.

With some of the profits from the arms sale, Marine Lieutenant Colonel Oliver North and other government officials arranged the purchase of weapons that were shipped secretly to Nicaragua. This action clearly violated the Boland Amendment.

When the public learned of the Iran-contra affair in 1986, a major scandal erupted. People were shocked to discover that illegal acts had been carried out by North and other officers of the National Security Council, a high-level White House agency that reports to the president about foreign and defense matters.

Televised congressional hearings probed into the

Iran-contra affair in 1987. Later ten government officials, including North, either were convicted or pleaded guilty in trials in which they were charged with criminal offenses.

President Reagan steadfastly claimed that he had not known about the use of funds from the Iranian weapons sale to help arm the contras. But if that was the case, many felt he was guilty of not insisting that his aides inform him of any actions that might embarrass his administration.

One of the most important achievements of the Reagan presidency was the improvement of American-Soviet relations. When Reagan entered the White House in 1981, he was chiefly concerned with increasing the military strength of the United States so that it definitely would be more powerful than the Soviet Union, which he called "the evil empire."[13] He continued to oppose the Communist system, but as the years passed he began to consider ways to ease tensions between the two superpowers. "The fact that neither of us likes the other system," he said in 1984, "is no reason to refuse to talk."[14]

President Reagan and Soviet leader Mikhail Gorbachev held four summit meetings between 1985 and 1988. At their first meeting, the two men agreed to promote educational, scientific, and cultural exchanges between their countries and discussed the possibility of reducing their stockpiles of nuclear weapons.

In 1987, Reagan and Gorbachev signed a treaty that called for the destruction of all ground-launched U.S. and Soviet nuclear missiles with ranges between 300 and 3,400 miles. When this treaty was enforced in 1988, it marked the first time during the forty-year Cold War that the actual number of nuclear weapons had been reduced.

Many presidents have found their job frustrating

and depressing. "If he knew what it entails," Harry Truman said in 1947, "no man in his right mind would ever want to be president."[15]

Ronald Reagan, however, enjoyed his presidency, which ended in 1989. "When I was announcing sports I was happy," he wrote, "and thought that was all I wanted out of life. Then came the chance at Hollywood, and that was even better. Now I'm doing something that makes everything else I've done seem as dull as dishwater."[16]

In 1994, when he was eighty-three years old, Reagan disclosed that he had Alzheimer's disease, a neurological disorder that weakens mental abilities and eventually kills many older adults. "I now will begin the journey that will lead me into the sunset of my life," he said. Then, in his typically optimistic way, he added, "I know that for America there will always be a bright dawn ahead."[17]

SOURCE NOTES

1

1. Richard M. Nixon, *RN: The Memoirs of Richard Nixon* (New York: Grosset and Dunlap, 1978), 10.

2. Dee Lillegard, *Richard Nixon* (Chicago: Childrens Press, 1988), 20.

3. Jonathan Aitken, *Nixon: A Life* (Washington, D.C.: Regnery, 1993), 21.

4. Fawn M. Brodie, *Richard Nixon: The Shaping of His Character* (New York: Norton, 1981), 45.

5. Julie Nixon Eisenhower, *Pat Nixon: The Untold Story* (New York: Simon and Schuster, 1986), 55.

6. *Time*, May 2, 1994, 45.

7. Ibid.

8. Richard M. Nixon, *Six Crises* (Garden City, N.Y.: Doubleday, 1962), 62.

9. Aitken, *Nixon: A Life*, 217.

10. Brodie, *Richard Nixon*, 463.

11. Edmund Lindop, *All About Republicans* (Hillside, N.J.: Enslow, 1985), 29.

12. David C. Whitney, *The American Presidents* (Garden City, N.Y.: Doubleday, 1985), 347.

13. Gerald R. Ford, *A Time to Heal* (New York: Harper and Row, 1979), 168.

14. Doris Faber and Harold Faber, *American Government: Great Lives* (New York: Scribners, 1988), 203.

2

1. Jimmy Carter, *A Government as Good as Its People* (New York: Simon and Schuster, 1977), 110.

2. Margaret Poynter, *The Jimmy Carter Story* (New York: Messner, 1978), 19.

3. Rosalynn Carter, *First Lady of Plains* (Boston: Houghton Mifflin, 1984), 23-24.

4. Ibid., 24.

5. Linda R. Wade, *James Carter* (Chicago: Childrens Press, 1989), 27.

6. Frank Freidel, *Our Country's Presidents* (Washington, D.C.: National Geographic Society, 1981), 267.

7. Jimmy Carter, *A Government as Good as Its People*, 14.

8. Richard Hyatt, *The Carters of Plains* (Huntsville, Ala.: Strode, 1977), 201.

9. Jimmy Carter, *A Government as Good as Its People*, 125.

10. David C. Whitney, *The American Presidents* (Garden City, N.Y.: Doubleday, 1985), 393.

11. Ibid., 398.

12. Jimmy Carter, *A Government as Good as Its People*, 117.

13. Jimmy Carter, *Keeping Faith: Memoirs of a President* (New York: Bantam, 1982), 155.

14. Walter LaFeber, *The American Age: United States Foreign Policy at Home and Abroad Since 1750* (New York: Norton, 1989), 665.

15. *Los Angeles Times,* February 10, 1995, section E, 4.

3

1. Ronald Reagan, *An American Life* (New York: Simon and Schuster, 1990), 260.

2. Ronald Reagan with Richard G. Hubler, *Where's the Rest of Me? The Ronald Reagan Story* (New York: Duell, Sloan, and Pearce, 1965), 3.

3. Anne Edwards, *Early Reagan* (New York: Morrow, 1987), 137.

4. Edmund Lindop, *All About Republicans*, 24.

5. Frank van der Linden, *The Real Reagan* (New York: Morrow, 1981), 58.

6. Nancy Reagan with Bill Libby, *Nancy* (New York: Morrow, 1980), 122.

7. Ronald Reagan, *An American Life*, 129.

8. Zachary Kent, *Ronald Reagan* (Chicago: Childrens Press, 1989), 53.

9. Lou Cannon, *President Reagan: The Role of a Lifetime* (New York: Simon and Schuster, 1991), 92.

10. Ibid., 116.

11. Lindop, *All About Republicans*, 25.

12. Walter LaFeber, *The American Age: United States Foreign Policy at Home and Abroad Since 1750*, 672.

13. Cannon, *President Reagan*, 57.

14. LaFeber, *The American Age*, 694.

15. *Time*, March 13, 1995, 68.

16. Lindop, *All About Republicans*, 26.

17. *Newsweek*, November 14, 1994, 38.

FURTHER READING

Beard, Charles A. *Charles A. Beard's the Presidents in American History*. Rev. ed. Englewood Cliffs, N.J.: Messner, 1989.

Blassingame, Wyatt. *The Look-It-Up Book of Presidents*. Rev. ed. New York: Random House, 1992.

Boller, Paul F., Jr. *Presidential Wives*. New York: Oxford University Press, 1988.

Carter, Jimmy. *A Government as Good as Its People*. New York: Simon and Schuster, 1977.

———. *Keeping Faith: Memoirs of a President*. New York: Bantam, 1982.

———. *Talking Peace: A Vision for the Next Generation*. New York: Dutton, 1993.

Coy, Harold. *The First Book of Presidents*. Rev. ed. New York: Franklin Watts, 1985.

Eisenhower, Julie Nixon. *Pat Nixon: The Untold Story*. New York: Simon and Schuster, 1986.

Faber, Doris, and Harold Faber. *American Government: Great Lives*. New York: Scribners, 1988.

Feinberg, Barbara Silberdick. *Watergate: Scandal in the White House*. New York: Franklin Watts, 1990.

Fox, Mary V. *The Story of Ronald Reagan*. Rev. ed. Hillside, N.J.: Enslow, 1986.

Friedman, Stanley P. *Ronald Reagan: His Life Story in Pictures*. New York: Dodd, Mead, 1986.

Garrison, Webb. *A Treasury of White House Tales*. Nashville: Rutledge Hills Press, 1989.

Hargrove, Jim. *Richard M. Nixon: The Thirty-seventh President*. Chicago: Childrens Press, 1985.

———. *The Story of Watergate*. Chicago: Childrens Press, 1988.

Kelly, C. Brian. *Best Little Stories From the White House*. Charlottesville, Va.: Montpelier Publishing, 1992.

Larsen, Rebecca. *Richard Nixon: Rise and Fall of a President*. New York: Franklin Watts, 1991.

Lawson, Don. *America Held Hostage: The Iran Hostage Crisis and the Iran-Contra Affair*. New York: Franklin Watts, 1991.

———. *The Picture Life of Ronald Reagan*. New York: Franklin Watts, 1981.

Lillegard, Dee. *Richard Nixon*. Chicago: Childrens Press, 1988.

Nixon, Richard M. *RN: The Memoirs of Richard Nixon*. New York: Grosset and Dunlap, 1978.

———. *Six Crises*. Garden City, N.Y.: Doubleday, 1962.

Pious, Richard. *The Presidency*. Columbus, Ohio: Silver Burdett, 1991.

Poynter, Margaret. *The Jimmy Carter Story*. New York: Messner, 1978.

Reagan, Nancy, with Bill Libby. *Nancy*. New York: Morrow, 1980.

Reagan, Ronald. *An American Life*. New York: Simon and Schuster, 1990.

Stein, R. Conrad. *The Powers of the President*. Chicago: Childrens Press, 1985.

Van der Linden, Frank. *The Real Reagan*. New York: Morrow, 1981.

Wade, Linda R. *James Carter*. Chicago: Childrens Press, 1989.

Walker, Barbara J. *The Picture Life of Jimmy Carter*. New York: Franklin Watts, 1977.

OTHER SOURCES OF INFORMATION

Basic American History, Program 2: Post–Civil War to the Present. Computer disks for both Apple and IBM. Grades 7 and up. Social Studies School Service, 10200 Jefferson Blvd., P.O. Box 802, Culver City, CA 90232.

Before Gorbachev: From Stalin to Brezhnev. Videocassette. Grades 7 and up. Filmic Archives, the Cinema Center, Botsford, CT 06404.

The Challenge of the Presidency (Nixon through Reagan). Videocassette. Grades 7 and up. Social Studies School Service, 10200 Jefferson Blvd, P.O. Box 802, Culver City, CA 90232.

The Civil Rights Movement: Witness to History. Videocassette. Grades 5 and up. Guidance Associates, P.O. Box 3000, Mt. Kisco, NY 10549.

The Eagle and the Bear: U.S.-Soviet Relations Since World War II. Videocassette or 4 filmstrips/4 audiocassettes. Grades 7 and up. Guidance Associates, P.O. Box 3000, Mt. Kisco, NY 10549.

First Ladies (since 1900). Videocassette. Grades 5–8. Filmic Archives, the Cinema Center, Botsford, CT 06404.

The Haldeman Diaries: Inside the White House. CD-ROM for Macintosh and Windows. Grades 7 and up. The Video Catalog, P.O. Box 64267, St. Paul, MN 55164.

Inside the White House. Videocassette. Grades 5–8. Filmic Archives, the Cinema Center, Botsford, CT 06404.

The Iran-Contra Arms Affair. Filmstrip/audiocassette. Grades 7 and up. New York Times. Social Studies School Service, 10200 Jefferson Blvd., P.O. Box 802, Culver City, CA 90232.

The Iron Curtain. Videocassette. Grades 5 and up. Britannica Learning Materials, 310 South Michigan Ave., Chicago, IL 60604.

Jimmy Carter, the Moralist President. Videocassette. Grades 7 and up. Social Studies School Service, 10200 Jefferson Blvd., P.O. Box 802, Culver City, CA 90232.

Modern America: The Primary Source, Volume 4. Photocopy masters of primary sources. Grades 7 and up. Perfection Form. Social Studies School Service, 10200 Jefferson Blvd., P.O. Box 802, Culver City, CA 90232.

Nixon: Checkers to Watergate. Videocassette. Grades 8 and up. Pyramid Film and Video, P.O. Box 1048, 2801 Colorado Ave., Santa Monica, CA 90406.

The Nixon Interviews With David Frost. Five videocassettes. Grades 7 and up. The Video Catalog, P.O. Box 64267, St. Paul, MN 55164.

Nixon: "Toughing It Out." Videocassette. Grades 6 and up. UPI Television News. Journal Films, 1560 Sherman Ave., Suite 100, Evanston, IL 60201.

Ordeal of Power: The President and the Presidency. Videocassette. Grades 7 and up. Guidance Associates, P.O. Box 3000, Mt. Kisco, NY 10549.

The Presidents. Videocassette. Grades 7 and up. Post Newsweek Section. Lucerne Media, 37 Ground Pine Road, Morris Plains, NJ 07950.

The Presidents: It All Started with George. CD-ROM for IBM. Grades 5 and up. National Geographic/IBM. National Geographic Education Services, P.O. Box 98019, Washington, DC 20090.

Presidents of the 20th Century. Videocassette. Grades 5–8. Filmic Archives, the Cinema Center, Botsford, CT 06404.

Reagan's Way. Videocassette. Grades 5 and up. MPI Home Video, 15825 Rob Roy Dr., Oak Forest, IL 60452.

The Reagan Years: In Pursuit of the American Dream. Videocassette. Grades 5 and up. MGM/UA Home Video, 10000 W. Washington Blvd., Culver City, CA 90232.

Richard Nixon. Videocassette. Grades 5 and up. WGBH Boston. Hearst Entertainment, 235 E. 45th Street, New York, NY 10017.

Ronald Reagan. Videocassette. Grades 5 and up. UPI Television News. Journal Films, 1560 Sherman Ave., Suite 100, Evanston, IL 60201.

Ronald Reagan and Richard Nixon on Camera. Videocassette. Grades 5 and up. Nostalgia Family Video, P.O. Box 606, Baker City, OR 97814.

Ronald Reagan: The Many Lives. Videocassette. Grades 5–8. Filmic Archives, the Cinema Center, Botsford, CT 06404.

U.S. History on CD-ROM. CD-ROM for both IBM and Macintosh. Grades 7 and up. Bureau Development, Inc. Social Studies School Service, 10200 Jefferson Blvd., P.O. Box 802, Culver City, CA 90232.

The Watergate Affair. Videocassette. Grades 6 and up. UPI Television News. Journal Films, 1560 Sherman Ave., Suite 100, Evanston, IL 60201.

Watergate: A Study of the Abuse of Presidential Power. Thirty-four photocopy masters or Apple computer disk. Grades 7 and up. Social Studies School Service, 10200 Jefferson Blvd., P.O. Box 802, Culver City, CA 90232.

Watergate: The Secret Story. Videocassette. Grades 8 and up. CBS. CBS/Fox Video, 1330 Avenue of the Americas, Fifth floor, New York, NY 10019.

We the People: The Presidency and the Constitution. (Includes interviews with Nixon, Ford, Carter, and Reagan.) Videocassette. Grades 7 and up. Trust for the Bicentennial of the Constitution/Close Up Foundation. Social Studies School Service, 10200 Jefferson Blvd., P.O. Box 802, Culver City, CA 90232.

INDEX